SUCCESSFUL COOKING

BBQ

INDEX

Contents

Barbecue Basics

Some barbecues can be as formal as a dinner party, others as relaxed as a picnic on the beach. Whatever the case, you will need to be prepared—choose the barbecue that suits you best, light the perfect fire and prepare the food to its maximum advantage.

TYPES OF BARBECUES

FUEL-BURNING

Fixed barbecue Many gardens contain some sort of fixture for barbecuing; they are relatively simple constructions, usually made from bricks or cement and featuring two grills – the bottom for building the fire, the top for cooking the food. These grills are not generally height-adjustable, so cooking can only be regulated by adjusting the fire, or moving the food away from or towards the fire. Being fixed these barbecues cannot, of course, be put out of high winds or moved to shelter in the event of rain. Despite this, fixed barbe-cues are easy to use and maintain, and quite often are large enough to cater for big gatherings.

Kettle barbecue One of the most popular styles of portable barbecue, the kettle barbecue features a close-fitting lid and air vents at top and bottom which allow for greater versatility and accuracy in cooking. They can function either as a traditional barbecue, as an oven or as a smoker. They only burn charcoal or heat beads (wood is not recommended) and are relatively small. The standard diameter is 57 cm (22 inches), so if barbecuing for large groups more than one barbecue is probably required.

Brazier This is the simplest style of fuel-burning barbecue, of which the small, cast iron hibachi is probably best known. A brazier consists of a shallow fire-box for burning fuel with a grill on top. Some grills are height adjustable or can rotate. Braziers are best fitted with a heat-reflecting hood, so that food will cook at an even temperature.

GAS OR ELECTRIC BARBECUES

Although often more expensive, these barbecues are very simple to use. They do not require an open flame, only connection to their heat source. In most cases, the gas or electricity heats a tray

A kettle barbecue can prepare a variety of foods.

A gas-fuelled wagon barbecue featuring hood and work areas.

Coals ready for cooking: Beads have developed a fine ash coating.

of reusable volcanic rock. Hickory chips can be placed over the rock-bed to produce a smoky flavour in the food, if desired. Sizes of models vary, the largest being the wagon style, which usually features a workbench, reflecting hood and, often, a bottom shelf for storage. While small portable gas models, which require only the connection of a gas bottle, are greatly manoeuvrable, electric models are, of course, confined to areas where mains electricity is available. Most gas or electric barbecues have temperature controls; their accuracy is their primary advantage. Electric models can be fitted with rotisseries or spit turners for spit roasting.

THE FIRE
FUEL
Although traditional, wood is not an ideal fuel for cooking. It can be difficult to light and burns with a flame. Charcoal or heat beads are preferable. They will create a bed of glowing heat which is perfect for cooking. They do not smell, smoke or flare and are readily available in supermarkets or hardware shops. (Heat beads are sometimes known as barbecue briquettes and should not be confused with heating briquettes, which are not suitable for cooking.)

Firelighters are essential for lighting charcoal or heat bead fires. They are soaked in kerosene so will ignite instantly. Do not attempt to cook while firelighters are still burning, as they give off kerosene fumes. Generally one or two firelighters will inflame about twenty pieces of charcoal or heat beads.

A 'normal' fire consists of about 50–60 heat beads or pieces of charcoal and will last for several hours. All recipes in this book can be cooked over a normal fire.

PREPARATION
Once lit, fires should be left to burn for about 40–50 minutes before cooking. Heat beads or charcoal will become pale and develop a fine, ash coating when they are ready to use. (Wood will have a low flame and have begun to char.) If preparing a kettle barbecue, leave off the lid while the fire is developing.

Build the fire in the middle of the grate, so that cooked food can be moved to the edge of the grill and kept warm.

TEMPERATURE CONTROL
A fire's temperature can be lowered by damping down with a spray of water. (A trigger-style plastic spray bottle is ideal.) Damping also produces steam which puts moisture back in the food.

The best and safest way to increase the heat of a fire is to add more fuel and wait for the fire to develop. Do not fan a fire to increase its heat; this will only produce a flame. Never pour flammable liquids on a fire.

COOKING TECHNIQUES
Most recipes in this book call for the food to be cooked over a direct flame. Recipes using indirect cooking are in Chapter 8. Indirect cooking is only possible on kettle barbecues.

DIRECT COOKING
As with frying in the kitchen, the less turning or handling of the food the better. Once the fire is ready, lightly brush the grill or flatplate with oil. Place the food over the hottest part of the fire and sear quickly on both sides; this retains moisture. Once seared, move the food to a cooler part of the grill or flatplate to cook for a few more minutes. Barbecuing is a fast-cooking process so even well-done food will not take very long. Techniques such as stir-frying are ideal for the barbecue flatplate.

Retain moistness in the meat by searing quickly and turning once only.

A barbecue flatplate can be used to stir-fry vegetables.

Test meat for 'doneness' by pressing gently with tongs.

Fish is ready when the flesh has turned opaque and flakes back easily.

Test meat for 'doneness' by firmly pressing it with tongs or the flat edge of a knife. Meat that is ready to serve should 'give' slightly but not resist pressure too easily. At first, the degree of doneness may be difficult to judge, but try to resist cutting or stabbing the meat; this not only reduces its succulence, but releases juices which may cause the fire to flare. Pork and chicken should not be served rare, so if in any doubt as to doneness remove to a separate plate and make a slight cut in the thickest part of the meat. If the juices do not run clear, return to the heat for further cooking. Test fish for

doneness by gently flaking back the flesh in the thickest part with a fork. Cooked flesh should be white and opaque, but still moist.

SMOKING

Smoking chips or chunks come from hickory wood, mesquite, dried mallee root, red-gum or acacia trees and are available from barbecue specialists and some hardware or variety stores. Their smoke provides an extra and unusual flavour to the food.

Smoking is best done on a covered barbecue but can also be done on an

open fire. Scatter smoking wood over the coals. Once the wood is burning, damp down with a little water to create more smoke. Smoking wood is available in chips and chunks; chips burn quickly so should be added towards the end of the cooking process. Chunks should last through the entire cooking process.

If glazing meat, such as ham, and smoking together, always glaze before adding wood. (Please note that some woods, such as pine, cedar or eucalyptus produce acrid smoke and are unsuitable for cooking. Use only wood sold specifically for smoking.)

RARE, MEDIUM OR WELL-DONE?

Not everybody likes their steak, beef or lamb cooked for the same length of time. Test for 'doneness' by gently pressing the meat with tongs or a flat-bladed knife. If in doubt, remove it from the barbecue and make a small cut in the meat to check its colour. Here is a guide to how the 5 classic degrees of 'doneness' should feel and look.

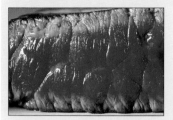

Bleu: Very soft to touch, red-raw inside, outer edge lightly cooked.

Rare: Soft to touch, red centre, thin edge of cooked meat.

Medium-rare: Springy to touch, with moist, pale-red centre.

Medium: Firm to touch, pink in centre and crisp, brown edges.

Well-done: Very firm to touch, brown outside and evenly cooked.

FLAVOURED BUTTERS

These butters add an interesting finishing touch to a meal and can be used instead of sauce. They are delicious on beef, pork, lamb, chicken, seafood and fish, as well as cooked vegetables or spread over hot bread.

Make 2 or 3 butters at a time and store, covered, in the refrigerator for up to 2 weeks. Butters can also be frozen and stored for several months. Shape butters into a log and simply slice off the required quantity, then return it to the refrigerator.

Alternatively, place butter in a piping bag and pipe individual servings over a piece of aluminium foil. Store, in refrigerator until required; place on food just before serving. Different flavoured butters can also be served in their own individual pots.

Always soften butter to room temperature before preparing.

GARLIC AND CHEESE BUTTER

Beat 100 g (3½ oz) each butter and softened cream cheese until light and creamy. Add 1 crushed garlic clove and 1 tablespoon each chopped fresh basil and chopped fresh parsley. Beat until smooth. Using plastic wrap, form into a log shape and refrigerate.

LIME AND CHILLI BUTTER

Beat 125 g (4½ oz) butter until light and creamy. Add 1 tablespoon lime juice, 1

Shape flavoured butter into a log, freeze and slice rounds as required.

A piping bag and a variety of nozzles can make interesting shapes.

Serving pots can be stored in the refrigerator for several weeks.

teaspoon grated lime rind, 1 teaspoon chopped chilli and 2 teaspoons chopped fresh coriander (cilantro). Beat until smooth. Using plastic wrap, form into a log shape and refrigerate.

SAVOURY ANCHOVY BUTTER

Combine 200 g (7 oz) butter, 4 drained anchovy fillets, 2 chopped spring onions (scallions), 1 garlic clove and 1 tablespoon grated lemon rind in food processor bowl. Process 30 seconds or until mixture forms a smooth paste. Transfer to small serving pots and refrigerate.

CAPSICUM AND TOMATO BUTTER

Cut 1 large red capsicum (pepper) in half; remove seeds and membrane. Brush skin with oil. Place under preheated grill (broiler) 5–10 minutes or until skin blackens. Cover with damp cloth and stand 5 minutes. Remove skin from capsicum; discard. Chop flesh roughly. Combine capsicum, 200 g (7

oz) chopped butter, 4 drained sun-dried tomatoes in oil and salt and pepper, to taste, in food processor bowl. Process 20–30 seconds or until smooth. Transfer to a serving bowl, cover in plastic wrap, and refrigerate.

MARINATING AND BASTING

Because food is cooked quickly on the barbecue, some foods should be marinated beforehand. Marinate food, preferably overnight, but at least a few hours ahead in a non-metal dish, covered, in the refrigerator; turn meat in marinade occasionally. Vinegar, citrus juice or wine-based marinades break down and tenderise the fibres of the meat, and are ideal for tougher meats.

Oil-based marinades moisturise meats and are suitable for meat such as chicken or pork. Yoghurt-based marinades are used with chicken or lamb, generally. The marinade will form a delicious crust over the meat when it is cooked.

Drain food from marinade and cook food as quickly as possible. If marinade is oil- or vinegar-based, reserve and use to baste.

Basting While not all foods need to be marinated before barbecuing, all should be basted during cooking. Basting seals moisture and prevents the food from sticking. Baste with olive oil or reserved marinade, lightly, on both sides. A pastry brush, or clean, unused paint-brush is ideal for this. Do not use a

Meat should be turned once or twice during marinating.

INDIRECT COOKING

Indirect cooking roasts or bakes food more slowly than direct cooking. It also allows for adding fragrant wood chips to the coals for added flavour.

To prepare a kettle barbecue for indirect cooking:

1. Remove lid; open bottom vent.
2. Position bottom grill inside bowl and attach charcoal rails. Heap coals in rails and position firelighters inside coals.
3. Light fire and allow coals to develop to fine-ash stage. (Leave lid off while fire develops.) Put a drip-tray or baking dish on bottom grill. Position top grill; add food.

To prepare a kettle barbecue for smoking:

1. Prepare barbecue as above.
2. When coals reach fine-ash stage, add wood chips; fill drip tray or baking dish with 1 litre (4 cups) hot water. Cover with lid until fragrant smoke develops.
3. Remove lid; centre food on top grill. Cover with lid.

Position two or three firelighters within the coals.

Light fire and allow the coals to develop.

Place a drip tray underneath top grill when coals are ready.

Spoon a generous quantity of smoking wood over hot coals.

brush with plastic bristles as the plastic may melt onto the food.

PLANNING YOUR BARBECUE

Design your menu to take full advantage of the barbecue – vegetables, kebabs, breads, even desserts can be cooked or warmed easily.

Serve at least 1 salad with the cooked food. Salad dressings and special sauces can be made in advance and stored in a screw-top jar in the refrigerator. Assemble salads up to 1 day in advance, but dress just before serving.

Light the fire about an hour before you are planning to use it; check the fire occasionally; it can easily go out if unattended.

Assemble all necessary utensils and accessories (for example, tongs, forks, knives, plates and basting brushes) before cooking.

Have plenty of snacks and drinks available for your guests, but place them well away from the fire.

Have a hose or water bottle standing by in case of emergencies. (As a general safety rule, do not attempt to barbecue in strong winds.) A torch may be useful if barbecuing at night.

Always extinguish a fire once you have finished cooking on it. If possible, clean out the barbecue as soon as it has cooled down; brush or scrape grills and flatplates, discard ash and embers.

Potatoes

TO COOK POTATOES

Wash and scrub the required amount of large old potatoes; pat dry with paper towels. Prick potatoes all over with a fork or skewer. Wrap potatoes individually in foil. Place potatoes around hot coals of barbecue or on top grill of a preheated kettle barbecue. Cook potatoes 30–60 minutes (depending on potato size). Insert a sharp knife or skewer in the centre to test if potato is cooked. (Flesh should be soft all the way through.) Remove foil from potatoes. Cut a large cross in the top of each. Squeeze to open; soften potato flesh by mashing gently with a fork. Mix a flavoured butter (such as garlic butter—see recipe below) into potato flesh and top with topping of choice. Serve hot.

Garlic Butter: (makes enough for 2 potatoes) Combine 50 g (1¾ oz) softened butter with 1–2 crushed garlic cloves. Mix well. Alternatively, add your favourite freshly chopped herbs or ground spices to butter to create your own flavoured butter.

CHICKEN AND CHEESE

Mix a small amount of garlic butter into potato flesh. Top each potato with grated cheddar cheese, shredded barbecued chicken, coleslaw, salt and pepper. Spoon over a dollop of sour cream. Sprinkle with sweet paprika. Serve hot.

MUSHROOM AND BACON

Heat 30 g (1 oz) butter in frying pan. Add 1 crushed garlic clove, 2 finely sliced bacon rashers. Cook 1 minute. Stir in 10 large sliced mushrooms. Cook 3–4 minutes until soft. Stir in 60 ml (¼ cup) cream and 1 tablespoon chopped chives. Season with salt and pepper. Cook 1 minute. Mix garlic butter into potato flesh. Spoon mixture over potato. Serve sprinkled with shavings of Parmesan cheese.

MEXICAN

Heat 1 tablespoon olive oil and 20 g (¼ oz) butter in medium pan. Add 1 finely chopped onion, 2 teaspoons dried mixed herbs, 1 crushed garlic clove, 1 teaspoon each ground cumin and coriander. Cook 2 minutes, or until onion is soft. Add 200 g (7 oz) lean minced (ground) beef, 2 tablespoons tomato paste (purée); cook 2–3 minutes. Stir in 1 chopped tomato, 55 g (¼ cup) canned red kidney beans, 60 ml (¼ cup) bottled tomato pasta sauce; season with salt, pepper and chilli powder. Simmer 5–10 minutes to reduce liquid. Spoon over hot potato. Top with grated Cheddar cheese, mashed avocado, sour cream and corn chips.

HERBED SOUR CREAM

Combine 250 ml (1 cup) sour cream, 1 tablespoon each of chopped chives, oregano and parsley, 2 teaspoons chopped mint, salt and pepper, to taste. Add 1 crushed garlic clove, if desired. Mix well. Spoon over hot potato.

Sauces

HORSERADISH CREAM

Using electric beaters, beat 125 g (4½ oz) cream cheese until soft and creamy. Add 1 tablespoon each of mayonnaise and sour cream, 1–2 teaspoons minced horseradish or horseradish cream and 1 tablespoon chopped chives, lemon thyme or parsley. Beat until combined. Serve with fish or beef.

CHILLI BARBECUE SAUCE

Heat 20 g (½ oz) butter in small pan. Add 1 teaspoon ground cumin, ½ teaspoon each of ground coriander and paprika. Cook 30 seconds. Stir in 1 tablespoon sweet chilli sauce, 80 ml (⅓ cup) bottled barbecue sauce and 2 teaspoons Worcestershire sauce. Mix well. Serve with lamb or beef.

CORIANDER MAYONNAISE

Place 3 egg yolks in food processor bowl or blender. With motor constantly running, add 185 ml (¾ cup) light olive oil in thin stream. Process until thick and creamy. Add 2 tablespoons lemon juice and 1–2 tablespoons chopped coriander (cilantro). Process until combined. Season. Add crushed garlic clove, or vary the taste with your own herb selection. Serve with chicken, fish or veal.

CREAMY MUSTARD SAUCE

Combine 2 tablespoons whole egg mayonnaise, 80 ml (⅓ cup) sour cream, 2–3 tablespoons Dijon or wholegrain mustard. Season with salt and pepper, to taste. Mix well. (Add 1 tablespoon of your favourite fresh chopped herbs, if desired.) If sauce is too thick, add a little cream to achieve required consistency. Serve with beef or chicken.

Dressings

HONEY GARLIC DRESSING
Combine 60 ml (¼ cup) peanut oil,
2 tablespoons lemon or lime juice,
1 teaspoon grated lemon zest,
6 teaspoons honey, 1–2 crushed garlic
cloves, 1 tablespoon fresh chopped
chives, salt and pepper, to taste, in
screwtop jar. Shake until well combined.
Pour over tossed green salad.

CREAMY DRESSING
Place 2 tablespoons olive oil, 1 tablespoon mayonnaise, 1 tablespoon
sour cream, 2 tablespoons lemon
juice, 1 teaspoon soft brown sugar,
salt and ground black pepper, to
taste, in a screwtop jar. Shake
until well combined. Pour over
Caesar salad. (Add 1 crushed garlic
clove and 1 tablespoon chopped
fresh chives to dressing, if desired.)

BASIL DRESSING

Combine 20 g (½ cup) basil leaves, ¾ teaspoon sugar, 1 garlic clove, 60 ml (¼ cup) olive or vegetable oil, 1 tablespoon white wine vinegar, 1 tablespoon grated Parmesan cheese, 40 g (¼ cup) toasted pinenuts, pepper and salt, to taste, in food processor bowl. Process until smooth. Add a little extra oil to thin, if necessary. Pour over tomato salad.

ORANGE AND SESAME DRESSING

Combine 1 tablespoon sesame oil, 2 tablespoons orange juice, 2 teaspoons toasted sesame seeds, 1 teaspoon grated orange zest, 1–2 teaspoons soy sauce, ¾ teaspoon grated ginger, salt and pepper, to taste, in screwtop jar. Shake until well combined. Pour over rocket (arugula) and watercress salad.

VINAIGRETTE DRESSING

Combine 60 ml (¼ cup) each of white wine vinegar and oil in a screwtop jar; season with salt and pepper, to taste. Shake until well combined. Pour over fresh garden salad. (Add 1–2 tablespoons of your favourite freshly chopped herbs to this dressing, if desired.)

Chilli Burger with Avocado Salsa

PREPARATION TIME: 25 minutes
TOTAL COOKING TIME: 10 minutes
SERVES 6

1 kg (2 lb 4 oz) minced (ground) beef
1 small onion, finely chopped
3 teaspoons chopped chilli
1 teaspoon ground cumin
2 tablespoons tomato paste (purée)
2 tablespoons chopped coriander (cilantro)
6 bread rolls
6 lettuce leaves

Avocado salsa
1 medium avocado
2 tablespoons lime juice
1 small tomato, chopped
130 g (4½ oz) can corn kernels, drained

1 Prepare and heat barbecue. Place beef in a large mixing bowl. Add onion, chilli, cumin, tomato paste and coriander. Using hands, mix until thoroughly combined. Divide mixture into 6 portions and shape into 1.5 cm (⅝ inch) thick patties.

2 Place patties on hot, lightly oiled grill or flatplate. Barbecue 5 minutes each side, turning only once. Serve between split bread rolls with lettuce and avocado salsa.

3 To make avocado salsa: Peel avocado and remove stone. Cut into small cubes, place in a bowl and toss immediately with lime juice. Add tomato and corn and lightly combine.

Combine beef, onion, chilli, cumin, tomato paste and coriander.

Grill patties for 5 minutes each side, turning only once.

Mix cubed avocado with lime juice, tomato and corn kernels.

Burger with the Works

PREPARATION TIME: 40 minutes
TOTAL COOKING TIME: 10–15 minutes
SERVES 6

750 g (1 lb 10 oz) lean minced (ground)
   beef
1 onion, finely chopped
1 egg
40 g (½ cup) fresh breadcrumbs
2 tablespoons tomato paste (purée)
1 tablespoon Worcestershire sauce
2 tablespoons chopped parsley
3 large onions
30 g (1 oz) butter
6 slices Cheddar cheese
6 eggs, extra
6 rashers bacon
6 large hamburger buns, lightly toasted
shredded lettuce
2 tomatoes, thinly sliced
6 large slices beetroot, drained
6 pineapple rings, drained
tomato sauce

1 Prepare and heat barbecue. Combine beef, onion, egg, breadcrumbs, tomato paste, Worcestershire sauce, parsley, salt and pepper in large bowl. Mix with hands until well combined.

2 Divide mixture into 6 portions. Shape each portion into round patties 1.5 cm (⅝ inch) thick. Cover and set aside. Slice onions into thin rings. Heat butter on hot barbecue flatplate. Cook onions, turning often until well browned. Move onions towards outer edge of flatplate to keep warm. Brush barbecue grill or flatplate liberally with oil.

3 Cook meat patties 3–4 minutes each side, or until browned and cooked through. Move patties to cooler part of barbecue or transfer to plate and keep warm. Place slice of cheese on each patty. (The heat of the burger will be enough to partially melt the cheese.) Heat a small amount of butter in a large frying pan. Fry eggs and bacon until eggs are cooked through and bacon is golden and crisp. Remove from heat. To assemble burgers: Place toasted bun bases on individual serving plates. Top each with lettuce, tomato, beetroot and pineapple. Place cooked meat patty on top, followed by cooked onions, egg, bacon and tomato sauce. Place remaining bun halves on top. Serve with potato chips, if desired.

Mix burger ingredients using your hands until well combined.

Shape beef mixture into patties 1.5cm thick.

Steak in Red Wine

PREPARATION TIME: 10 minutes
+ 3 hours marinating
TOTAL COOKING TIME: 5–10 minutes
SERVES 4

750 g (1 lb 10 oz) rump steak
250 ml (1 cup) good-quality red wine
2 teaspoons garlic salt
1 tablespoon dried oregano leaves

1 Cut steaks into large, even-sized serving pieces. Trim excess fat and sinew from meat.

2 Combine wine, salt, oregano leaves and pepper in a jug. Place steak in a large, shallow non-metal dish and pour on the marinade. Cover and refrigerate several hours or overnight. Prepare and heat barbecue 1 hour before cooking.

3 Cook steak on hot lightly greased barbecue grill on flatplate 3–4 minutes each side, or until cooked as desired, brushing with wine mixture frequently. Serve with potato salad and corn on the cob, if desired.

Trim serving-sized pieces of steak of any fat or sinew.

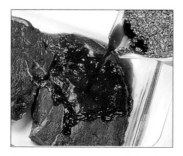

Place steaks in a non-metal dish and pour over marinade.

Brush steaks with wine marinade frequently while cooking.

Lamb Chops with Pineapple Salsa

PREPARATION TIME: 20 minutes
TOTAL COOKING TIME: 10 minutes
SERVES 6

12 lamb loin chops
2 tablespoons oil
1 teaspoon ground black pepper

Pineapple salsa
½ ripe pineapple (or 400 g/14 oz drained canned pineapple)
1 large red onion
1 fresh red chilli
1 tablespoon cider or rice vinegar
1 teaspoon sugar
2 tablespoons chopped mint

1 Prepare and heat barbecue. Trim meat of excess fat and sinew. Brush chops with oil and season with black pepper.

2 To make pineapple salsa: Peel pineapple; remove core and eyes. Cut into small cubes. Peel onion, finely chop. Slit open chilli, scrape out seeds. Chop chilli flesh finely. Combine pineapple, onion and chilli in medium bowl; mix lightly. Add vinegar, sugar, salt, pepper and mint; mix well.

3 Place lamb chops on lightly greased barbecue grill or flatplate. Cook chops 2–3 minutes each side, turning once, until just tender. Serve with pineapple salsa, baked potatoes and green salad, if desired.

Brush lamb loin chops with oil and season with black pepper.

Scrape seeds from chilli, mince, and combine with salsa ingredients.

Cook lamb chops for 2–3 minutes each side. Serve with salsa.

Tangy Beef Ribs

PREPARATION TIME: 20 minutes
+ 3 hours marinating
TOTAL COOKING TIME: 15–20 minutes
SERVES 4

1 kg (2 lb 4 oz) beef ribs
125 ml (½ cup) tomato sauce
2 tablespoons Worcestershire sauce
2 tablespoons soft brown sugar
1 teaspoon paprika
¼ teaspoon chilli powder
1 garlic clove, crushed

1 Chops ribs into individual serving pieces, if necessary. Bring a large pan of water to boil.

2 Cook ribs in boiling water for 5 minutes; drain.

3 Combine the tomato sauce, Worcestershire sauce, sugar, paprika, chilli powder and garlic in large bowl and mix well. Add ribs to sauce. Cover and marinate, in refrigerator, several hours or overnight. Prepare and heat barbecue 1 hour before cooking.

4 Cook ribs on hot lightly greased barbecue grill or flatplate 10–15 minutes, brushing frequently with marinade, or until ribs are well browned and cooked through. Serve with favourite barbecued vegetables or slices of grilled fresh pineapple, if desired.

Cook ribs in boiling water for 5 minutes, then drain.

Combine sauce ingredients, then add ribs and leave to marinate.

Brush ribs frequently with marinade while cooking.

Barbecued Hotdogs with Creamy Slaw

PREPARATION TIME: 20 minutes
TOTAL COOKING TIME: 10 minutes
SERVES 6

6 large, thick, spicy frankfurts
1 tablespoon oil
6 hotdog rolls
6 small lettuce leaves

Creamy slaw
100 g (3½ oz) red cabbage
100 g (3½ oz) green cabbage
2 spring onions (scallions)
125 g (½ cup) whole egg mayonnaise
1 tablespoon German mustard

1 Prepare and heat barbecue. Make 4 diagonal cuts in each frankfurt, slicing halfway through. Brush frankfurts with oil, and cook on hot, lightly oiled barbecue flatplate 7–10 minutes, or until cooked through.

2 Split rolls lengthways through the centre top; line with lettuce leaf. Place creamy slaw on lettuce, and top with hot dog. Serve immediately.

3 To make creamy slaw: Finely shred cabbage; finely chop spring onions. Combine mayonnaise with mustard. Place all ingredients in mixing bowl and toss to combine.

Make 4 diagonal cuts in each frankfurt, slicing halfway through.

Split hotdog rolls lengthways through the centre top.

Shred cabbage; mix with spring onions, mayonnaise and mustard.

Sweet and Sour Marinated Pork Kebabs

PREPARATION TIME: 30 minutes
+ 3 hours marinating
TOTAL COOKING TIME: 20 minutes
SERVES 6

1 kg (2 lb 4 oz) pork fillets
1 large red capsicum (pepper)
1 large green capsicum (pepper)
425 g (15 oz) can pineapple pieces
250 ml (1 cup) orange juice
60 ml (¼ cup) white vinegar
2 tablespoons soft brown sugar
2 teaspoons chilli garlic sauce
2 teaspoons cornflour (cornstarch)

1 Trim pork of excess fat and sinew. Cut meat into 2.5 cm (1 inch) cubes. Cut both capsicum into 2 cm (¾ inch) squares. Drain pineapple and reserve juice. Thread meat, alternately with capsicum and pineapple, onto skewers. Combine reserved pineapple juice with orange juice, vinegar, sugar and sauce. Place kebabs in a shallow non-metal dish, pour half the juice mixture over. Refrigerate, covered with plastic wrap, several hours or overnight, turning occasionally. Prepare and heat barbecue 1 hour before cooking.

2 To make sweet and sour sauce: Place remaining marinade in small pan. Mix cornflour with 1 table-spoon of the marinade in small bowl until smooth; add to pan. Stir over medium heat until mixture boils and thickens; transfer to small serving bowl. Cover surface with plastic wrap; leave to cool.

3 Place meat on a hot lightly oiled barbecue grill or flatplate and cook 15 minutes, turning occasionally, until tender. Serve kebabs with sweet and sour sauce.

Thread pork, pineapple and capsicum onto skewers.

Stir sweet and sour sauce over medium heat until it thickens.

Barbecue kebabs for 15 minutes, turning occasionally.

Herb and Garlic Sausage with Red Onion Relish

PREPARATION TIME: 20 minutes
TOTAL COOKING TIME: 40 minutes
SERVES 4

4 herb and garlic sausages
25 cm (10 inch) square focaccia
4 lettuce leaves, shredded
1 medium tomato, sliced

Red Onion Relish
2 tablespoons olive oil
2 medium red onions, sliced
2 teaspoons malt vinegar
1 tablespoon sugar

1 Prepare and heat barbecue. Place sausages on hot, lightly oiled barbecue grill or flatplate. Barbecue, turning frequently, 10 minutes, or until well browned and cooked through. Cut sausages in half, lengthways.

2 Cut focaccia into quarters, split in half horizontally and toast under a preheated grill (broiler) each side until golden. Place lettuce and tomato on each focaccia base, followed by sausage. Top with red onion relish. Cover with the remaining focaccia squares.

3 To make red onion relish: Heat oil in medium pan, cook onions over medium–low heat 15 minutes, stirring frequently, until very soft but not browned. Add vinegar and sugar; cook a further 10 minutes. Serve warm or at room temperature.

Cook sausages for 10 minutes until browned and cooked through.

Toast focaccia under grill until golden.

Cook red onions over medium-low heat until very soft.

Ginger-orange Pork Steaks

PREPARATION TIME: 15 minutes
+ 3 hours marinating
TOTAL COOKING TIME: 20 minutes
SERVES 6

6 pork butterfly steaks (200 g/
  7 oz each)
250 ml (1 cup) ginger wine
160 g (½ cup) orange marmalade
2 tablespoons oil
1 tablespoon grated ginger

1 Trim pork steaks of excess fat and sinew. Combine wine, marmalade, oil and ginger in small jug; mix well. Place steaks in shallow non-metal dish; pour marinade over. Store, covered with plastic wrap, in refrigerator several hours or overnight, turning occasionally. Prepare and heat barbecue 1hour before cooking. Drain pork steaks; reserve marinade.

2 Place pork on hot, lightly oiled barbecue grill or flatplate. Cook 5 minutes each side or until tender, turning once.

3 While meat is cooking, place reserved marinade in small pan. Bring to the boil; reduce heat and simmer 5 minutes until marinade has reduced and thickened slightly. Pour over pork steaks immediately.

Place pork steaks in non-metal dish and pour marinade over.

Cook pork steaks for 5 minutes each side until tender.

Simmer reserved marinade until it has reduced and thickened.

Beef Satay Sticks with Peanut Sauce

PREPARATION TIME: 30 minutes
+ 3 hours marinating
TOTAL COOKING TIME: 10–15 minutes
SERVES 4

800 g (1 lb 12 oz) rump steak
80 ml (⅓ cup) soy sauce
2 tablespoons oil
2 garlic cloves, crushed
1 teaspoon grated ginger

Peanut sauce
250 ml (1 cup) pineapple juice
250 g (1 cup) peanut butter
½ teaspoon garlic powder
½ teaspoon onion powder
2 tablespoons sweet chilli sauce
60 ml (¼ cup) soy sauce

1 Trim steak of excess fat and sinew. Slice meat across the grain evenly into long, thin strips. Thread meat strips onto skewers, bunching them thickly along three-quarters of the skewer; place satays in a shallow non-metal dish.

2 Combine soy sauce, oil, garlic and ginger in a small jug: pour over satays. Store in refrigerator, covered with plastic wrap, several hours or overnight, turning occasionally. Prepare and heat barbecue 1 hour before cooking. Place skewers on hot, lightly oiled grill or flatplate. Barbecue 8–10 minutes, or until tender, turning occasionally. Serve with peanut sauce.

3 To make peanut sauce: Combine pineapple juice, peanut butter, garlic and onion powders and sauces in a small pan and stir over medium heat 5 minutes, or until smooth. Serve warm.

Trim steak of any excess fat and cut into thin strips.

Thread steak strips onto skewers and pour soy sauce marinade over.

Combine peanut sauce ingredients and stir over medium heat.

Cheese-stuffed Burger with Red Salsa

PREPARATION TIME: 25 minutes
+ 1 hour standing
TOTAL COOKING TIME: 20 minutes
SERVES 6

1 kg (2 lb 4 oz) minced (ground) beef
1 small onion, finely chopped
2 tablespoons chopped parsley
1 teaspoon dried oregano
1 tablespoon tomato paste (purée)
70 g (2½ oz) Cheddar cheese
6 white bread rolls
lettuce leaves

Red salsa
2 red capsicums (peppers)
1 medium ripe tomato, finely chopped
1 small red onion, finely chopped
1 tablespoon olive oil
2 teaspoons red wine vinegar

1 Prepare and heat barbecue. Place beef in large mixing bowl; add onion, herbs and tomato paste. Using hands, mix until thoroughly combined. Divide mixture into 6 equal portions and shape into patties. Cut cheese into small squares. Make a cavity in the top of each patty with thumb. Place cheese in cavity and smooth mince over to enclose the cheese completely.

2 Place patties on hot, lightly oiled barbecue grill or flatplate. Barbecue 4–5 minutes each side, turning once. Remove from barbecue; keep warm. Split each roll in half; place a lettuce leaf on the base of each, top with pattie and red salsa.

3 To make red salsa: Trim capsicums, remove seeds and membrane. Cut into wide pieces and place skin-side up under a hot grill (broiler). Cook 4–5 minutes, or until skin blisters and blackens. Cover with damp tea towel and leave to cool. Remove skin from capsicum and finely chop flesh. Combine with tomato, onion, olive oil and vinegar and stand at least 1 hour to allow flavours to develop. Serve at room temperature.

Make a cavity in each patty and place cheese square inside patty.

Barbecue patties for 4–5 minutes each side, turning once.

Cook capsicum until skin blackens and blisters. Cool and remove skin.

Apricot Glazed Sausages and Onions

PREPARATION TIME: 20 minutes
TOTAL COOKING TIME: 15–20 minutes
SERVES 4–6

3 onions
8 thick beef sausages
1 teaspoon seeded mustard
180 g (1 cup) dried apricot halves
185 ml (¾ cup) apricot nectar

1 Prepare and heat barbecue. Cut onions in half; slice thinly. Cook onions on lightly greased barbecue flat-plate 5 minutes, or until soft. Transfer to a plate; keep warm. Place sausages on barbecue flatplate and cook 5 minutes, or until well browned, turning frequently.

2 Slice sausages lengthways, three-quarters of the way through. Cook, cut-side down, a further 5 minutes, or until browned. Add mustard, apricots and onions to sausages; stir.

3 Add nectar to sausage, apricot and onion mixture, a little at a time. Stir until nectar coats the sausages and begins to thicken. Repeat this process until all nectar is used. Serve sausages cut-side up, topped with onion and apricot mixture.

Cut onions in half and slice thinly.

Slice sausages lengthways, three-quarters of the way through.

Add apricot and onion mixture to sausages, a little at a time.

Lamb Kofta Kebabs with Tahini Dressing

PREPARATION TIME: 25 minutes
TOTAL COOKING TIME: 10 minutes
SERVES 4–6

600 g (1 lb 5 oz) lean lamb
1 medium onion, roughly chopped
2 garlic cloves, roughly chopped
1 teaspoon ground black pepper
1½ teaspoons ground cumin
½ teaspoon ground cinnamon
1 teaspoon sweet paprika
1 teaspoon salt
2 slices bread, crusts removed, quartered
1 egg, lightly beaten
olive oil, for coating

Tahini dressing
2 tablespoons tahini (sesame paste)
3 teaspoons lemon juice
1 small garlic clove, crushed
2 tablespoons sour cream
1 tablespoon chopped parsley

1 Trim meat of any excess fat and sinew. Cut into small pieces suitable for processing. Prepare and heat barbecue.

2 Place lamb, onion, garlic, pepper, cumin, cinnamon, paprika, salt, bread and egg in food processor bowl. Process 20–30 seconds, or until mixture becomes a smooth paste.

3 Divide mixture into 12. Using oil-coated hands, shape portions into sausages. Wrap sausages around skewers; refrigerate until needed.

4 To make tahini dressing: Combine tahini, lemon juice, garlic, sour cream, chopped parsley, pinch of salt and 2–3 tablespoons water in small bowl. Stir until creamy.

5 Arrange kofta kebabs on hot, lightly greased barbecue grill or flatplate. Cook 10 minutes, turning frequently, until browned and cooked through. Serve with tahini dressing and grilled tomato halves, if desired.

Process kofta ingredients until mixture becomes a smooth paste.

Divide mixture into 12 portions and shape into sausages.

Combine tahini dressing ingredients and stir until creamy.

Best-ever Burger with Homemade Barbecue Sauce

PREPARATION TIME: 20 minutes + refrigeration
TOTAL COOKING TIME: 25 minutes
SERVES 6

750 g (1 lb 10 oz) minced (ground) beef
250 g (9 oz) minced (ground) sausage
1 small onion, finely chopped
1 tablespoon Worcestershire sauce
2 tablespoons tomato sauce
80 g (1 cup) fresh breadcrumbs
1 egg, lightly beaten
2 large onions, extra, thinly sliced in rings
6 wholemeal rolls
6 small lettuce leaves
1 large tomato, sliced

Homemade barbecue sauce
2 teaspoons oil
1 small onion, finely chopped
3 teaspoons brown vinegar
1 tablespoon soft brown sugar
80 ml (⅓ cup) tomato sauce
2 teaspoons Worcestershire sauce
2 teaspoons soy sauce

1 Place minced beef and sausage mince in a large bowl. Add onion, sauces, breadcrumbs and egg. Using hands, mix until thoroughly combined. Divide mixture into 6 equal portions and shape into 1.5 cm (¼ inch) thick patties. Refrigerate patties at least 30 minutes. Prepare and heat barbecue.

2 Place patties on hot, lightly oiled barbecue grill or flatplate. Barbecue over hottest part of fire 8 minutes each side, turning once. While patties are cooking, fry onions on oiled flatplate until golden.

4 To assemble burgers: Split rolls in half. Place bases on individual serving plates. Top each base with lettuce leaf, patty, tomato slice and fried onions. Top with a generous quantity of homemade barbecue sauce. Cover with remaining bun half.

5 To make homemade barbecue sauce: Heat oil in a small pan. Cook onion 5 minutes, or until soft. Add vinegar, sugar and sauces; stir to combine and bring to the boil. Reduce heat and simmer 3 minutes. Cool.

Shape minced beef and sausage mixture into patties.

Cook onion, then add other sauce ingredients and simmer.

Honey Glazed Chicken Breasts

PREPARATION TIME: 6 minutes
+ 20 minutes marinating
TOTAL COOKING TIME: 10 minutes
SERVES 6

6 chicken breast fillets (1 kg/2 lb 4 oz)
50 g (1¾ oz) butter, softened
60 ml (¼ cup) honey
60 ml (¼ cup) barbecue sauce
2 teaspoons seeded mustard

1 Trim chicken of excess fat and sinew. Remove skin.

2 Use a sharp knife to make three or four diagonal slashes across one side of each chicken breast. Prepare and heat barbecue.

3 Combine butter, honey, barbecue sauce and mustard in a small bowl. Spread half of the marinade thickly over the slashed side of the chicken; cover. Set remaining marinade aside. Stand chicken at room temperature 20 minutes.

4 Place chicken breasts, slashed-side up, on hot, lightly greased grill or flatplate. Cook 2–3 minutes each side or until tender. Brush with reserved marinade several times during cooking. Serve hot with buttered ribbon noodles, if desired.

Make 3 or 4 diagonal slashes across one side of chicken breasts.

Combine butter, honey, barbecue sauce and mustard in a bowl.

Brush chicken pieces with sauce several times while cooking.

Middle Eastern Baked Chicken

PREPARATION TIME: 30 minutes
TOTAL COOKING TIME: 1 hour 15 minutes
SERVES 6

1.6 kg (3 lb 8 oz) chicken
125 ml (½ cup) boiling water
95 g (½ cup) instant couscous
4 pitted dates, chopped
4 dried apricots, chopped
1 tablespoon lime juice
1 tablespoon olive oil
20 g (½ oz) butter
1 medium onion, chopped
1–2 garlic cloves, chopped
1 teaspoon salt
¼ teaspoon ground black pepper
1 teaspoon ground coriander
2 tablespoons chopped parsley
salt and pepper, extra
1 teaspoon ground cumin
1 tablespoon olive oil, extra

1 Prepare and heat kettle barbecue for indirect cooking. Place drip tray underneath top grill.

2 Remove giblets and any large deposits of fat from chicken. Wipe and pat dry chicken with paper towel. Pour boiling water over couscous and set aside 15 minutes for couscous to swell and soften. Soak dates and apricots in lime juice; set aside.

3 Heat oil and butter in pan, add onion and garlic; cook 3–4 minutes until translucent. Remove from heat; add couscous and soaked dried fruit, salt, pepper, coriander and parsley. Mix well. Spoon stuffing into chicken cavity and close with tooth-picks or a skewer. Tie legs together with string.

4 Rub chicken skin all over with combined salt, pepper, cumin and extra oil. Place chicken in the centre of a large piece of greased foil and wrap.

5 Place the parcel on barbecue grill over drip tray. Cover barbecue, cook 50 minutes. Open the foil, crimping the edges to form a tray. Cook a further 20 minutes, or until chicken is golden. Remove from heat and stand 5–6 minutes before carving.

Remove giblets and any large deposits of fat from chicken.

When couscous is soft and swollen, add other stuffing ingredients.

Open foil during last 20 minutes of cooking to allow skin to crisp.

Chicken Burger with Tangy Garlic Mayonnaise

PREPARATION TIME: 20 minutes
+ 3 hours marinating
TOTAL COOKING TIME: 15 minutes
SERVES 4

4 chicken breast fillets
125 ml (½ cup) lime juice
1 tablespoon sweet chilli sauce
4 bacon rashers
4 hamburger buns
4 lettuce leaves
1 large tomato, sliced

Garlic Mayonnaise
2 egg yolks
2 garlic cloves, crushed
1 tablespoon Dijon mustard
1 tablespoon lemon juice
125 ml (½ cup) olive oil

1 Place chicken in a shallow non-metal dish; prick chicken breasts with a skewer several times.

Combine lime juice and chilli sauce in a jug. Pour over chicken; cover. Marinate several hours or overnight. Prepare and light barbecue 1 hour before cooking. Remove and discard rind from bacon, cut bacon in half crossways.

2 Place chicken and bacon on hot lightly greased barbecue grill or flatplate. Cook bacon 5 minutes, or until crisp. Cook chicken another 7 minutes until well browned and cooked through, turning once. Cut hamburger buns in half and toast each side until lightly browned. Top bases with lettuce, tomato, chicken and bacon. Top with garlic mayonnaise; finish with remaining bun top.

3 To make garlic mayonnaise: Place egg yolks, garlic, mustard and lemon juice in food processor bowl or blender. Process until smooth. With motor constantly running, add the oil in a thin, steady stream. Process until mayonnaise reaches a thick consistency. Refrigerate, covered, until required.

Place chicken in a non-metal tray and pour over lime and chilli sauce.

Add oil to mayonnaise ingredients in a thin, steady stream.

Citrus Chicken Drumsticks

PREPARATION TIME: 20 minutes
+ 3 hours marinating
TOTAL COOKING TIME: 20 minutes
SERVES 4

8 chicken drumsticks
80 ml (⅓ cup) orange juice
80 ml (⅓ cup) lemon juice
1 teaspoon grated orange zest
1 teaspoon grated lemon zest
1 teaspoon sesame oil
1 tablespoon olive oil
1 spring onion (scallion), finely chopped

1 Wash drumsticks and pat dry with paper towels. Trim any excess fat and score thickest part of chicken with a knife. Place in a shallow non-metal dish.

2 Combine juices, zests, oils and spring onion in jug, pour over chicken. Store, covered with plastic wrap, in refrigerator several hours or overnight, turning occasionally. Drain chicken, reserve marinade. Prepare and heat barbecue 1 hour before cooking.

3 Cook drumsticks on hot lightly oiled barbecue grill or flatplate 15–20 minutes, or until tender. Brush occasionally with the reserved marinade. Serve immediately.

Score thickest part of chicken drumsticks with a sharp knife.

Pour marinade over chicken and leave to marinate.

Brush chicken occasionally with marinade while cooking.

Chicken Fajitas

PREPARATION TIME: 35 minutes
+ 3 hours marinating
TOTAL COOKING TIME: 10 minutes
SERVES 4

4 chicken breast fillets
2 tablespoons olive oil
60 ml (¼ cup) lime juice
2 garlic cloves, crushed
1 teaspoon ground cumin
15 g (¼ cup) chopped fresh coriander
  (cilantro) leaves
8 flour tortillas
1 tablespoon olive oil, extra
2 medium onions, sliced
2 medium green capsicum (pepper), cut into
  thin strips
125 g (1 cup) grated Cheddar cheese
1 large avocado, sliced
250 ml (1 cup) bottled tomato salsa

1 Trim chicken of fat and sinew. Cut chicken into thin strips. Place in shallow non-metal dish. Combine oil, juice, garlic, cumin and coriander in jug; mix well. Pour over chicken. Store, covered, in the refrigerator several hours or overnight. Prepare and heat barbecue 1 hour before cooking.

2 Wrap tortillas in foil and place on a cool part of the barbecue grill for 10 minutes to warm through. Heat oil on flatplate. Cook onion and capsicum for 5 minutes or until soft. Push over to a cooler part of the plate to keep warm.

3 Place chicken and marinade on flatplate and cook 5 minutes until just tender. Transfer chicken, vegetables and wrapped tortillas to serving platter. Make up individual fajitas by placing chicken, cooked onion and capsicum, grated cheese and avocado over flat tortillas. Top with salsa. Roll up to enclose filling.

Mix lime juice, garlic, cumin and coriander and pour over chicken.

Cook onion and capsicum for 5 minutes, until soft.

Cook chicken together with marinade and transfer to serving plate.

Teriyaki Chicken Wings

PREPARATION TIME: 15 minutes
+ 3 hours marinating
TOTAL COOKING TIME: 13 minutes
SERVES 4

8 chicken wings
60 ml (¼ cup) soy sauce
2 tablespoons sherry
2 teaspoons grated ginger
1 garlic clove, crushed
1 tablespoon honey

1 Wash chicken wings and pat dry with paper towel. Trim any excess fat from wings, and tuck tips under to form a triangle.

2 Place wings in shallow non-metal dish. Combine soy sauce, sherry, ginger, garlic and honey in a jug; mix well. Pour over chicken. Store, covered with plastic wrap, in refrigerator several hours or overnight. Prepare and light barbecue 1 hour before cooking. Lightly brush two sheets of aluminium foil with oil. Place 4 wings in a single layer on each piece of foil; wrap completely.

3 Place parcels on hot barbecue grill or flatplate 10 minutes. Remove parcels from heat; unwrap. Place wings directly on lightly greased grill 3 minutes, or until brown. Turn wings frequently and brush with any remaining marinade.

Wash and trim chicken wings, and tuck tip under to form triangle

Place 4 wings on sheet of foil, and wrap to enclose.

Cook in foil for 10 minutes, then place wings directly on grill.

Salmon Cutlets with Fruit Salsa

PREPARATION TIME: 20 minutes
+ 3 hours marinating
TOTAL COOKING TIME: 10 minutes
SERVES 4

4 salmon cutlets
6 teaspoons seasoned pepper
2 tablespoons lemon juice
125 ml (½ cup) lime juice
1 tablespoon chopped fresh thyme

Fruit salsa
½ small pawpaw, peeled
¼ small pineapple, peeled
3 spring onions (scallions), chopped
1 tablespoon chopped fresh coriander
  (cilantro)
2 tablespoons lime juice
3 teaspoons caster (superfine) sugar
salt, to taste

1 Sprinkle salmon cutlets all over with seasoned pepper. Place salmon cutlets in shallow non-metal dish. Combine lemon juice, lime juice and thyme in small jug. Pour over salmon cutlets. Cover and refrigerate several hours.

2 Place salmon on hot, lightly greased barbecue grill or flatplate; brush with any remaining marinade. Cook 5–10 minutes each side, turning once, until outside is lightly browned and flesh is just cooked on the inside. Serve with fruit salsa.

3 To make fruit salsa: Chop pawpaw and pineapple into 1 cm (½ inch) cubes. Combine in medium bowl with spring onions, coriander, lime juice, caster sugar and salt.

Combine lemon and lime juices and thyme and pour over salmon.

Cook salmon until outside is lightly browned and just cooked.

Combine salsa ingredients and serve with salmon.

Cajun Calamari

PREPARATION TIME: 15 minutes
+ 3 hours marinating
TOTAL COOKING TIME: 5 minutes
SERVES 4

600 g (1 lb 5 oz) large calamari (or squid)
  hoods
60 ml (¼ cup) lemon juice
2 garlic cloves, crushed
2 teaspoons tomato paste (purée)
1 teaspoon garam masala
2 teaspoons ground coriander
2 teaspoons paprika
2 teaspoons seasoned pepper
2 teaspoons caster (superfine) sugar
1 tablespoon grated fresh ginger
1 tablespoon olive oil
¼ teaspoon ground nutmeg
pinch chilli powder

1 Wash calamari thoroughly, removing any membrane. Pat dry with paper towel. Using a sharp knife, cut through one side of each hood, open out to give a large, flat piece of flesh. With inside facing up, score flesh diagonally, in a criss-cross pattern, taking care not to cut all the way through. Against the grain of those cuts, slice flesh into long strips about 2 cm (¾ inch) thick.

2 Combine juice, garlic, tomato paste, spices, sugar, ginger, oil, nutmeg and chilli in bowl; mix well. Add calamari strips; stir to combine. Cover and refrigerate several hours or overnight. Prepare and heat barbecue 1 hour before cooking.

3 Cook calamari and marinade on hot, lightly greased barbecue flatplate 5 minutes or until flesh curls and turns white. Remove from the heat and serve immediately.

Score calamari flesh diagonally in a criss-cross pattern.

Add calamari strips to marinade, stir to combine, and refrigerate.

Cook calamari together with marinade until flesh curls.

Garlic King Prawns

PREPARATION TIME: 10 minutes
+ 3 hours marinating
TOTAL COOKING TIME: 5 minutes
SERVES 4

500 g (1 lb 2 oz) raw king prawns (shrimp)

Marinade
2 tablespoons lemon juice
2 tablespoons sesame oil
2 garlic cloves, crushed
2 teaspoons grated fresh ginger

1 Remove heads from prawns. Peel and devein prawns, leaving tails intact. (Reserve the heads and shell for fish stock, if you like.) Make a cut in the prawn body, slicing three-quarters of the way through the flesh from head to tail.

2 To make marinade: Combine juice, oil, garlic and ginger in jug; mix well.

3 Place prawns in bowl; pour on marinade and mix well. Cover and refrigerate several hours or overnight. Prepare and light barbecue 1 hour before cooking.

4 Cook prawns on hot, lightly greased flatplate 3–5 minutes, or until pink in colour and cooked through. Brush frequently with marinade while cooking. Serve immediately.

Shell and devein prawns, leaving tails intact.

Combine lemon juice, oil, garlic and ginger and pour over prawns.

Cook prawns on a hot barbecue until pink in colour.

Fish Patties

PREPARATION TIME: 25 minutes
TOTAL COOKING TIME: 10 minutes
MAKES 8–10 patties

750 g (1 lb 10 oz) white fish fillets, cut into
  cubes
100 g (1 cup) stale white breadcrumbs
3 spring onions (scallions), chopped
60 ml (¼ cup) lemon juice
2 teaspoons seasoned pepper
1 tablespoon chopped fresh dill
2 tablespoons chopped parsley
90 g (¾ cup) grated Cheddar cheese
1 egg
60 g (½ cup) plain (all-purpose) flour, for
  dusting

Herbed mayonnaise
125 ml (½ cup) mayonnaise
1 tablespoon chopped fresh parsley
1 tablespoon chopped fresh chives
2 teaspoons chopped capers

1 Prepare and heat barbecue. Place fish in food processor bowl. Process 20–30 seconds until smooth.

2 Place minced fish in large bowl. Add breadcrumbs, spring onions, juice, pepper, herbs, cheese and egg. Mix well. Divide into 8–10 portions. Shape into round patties. Place on tray and refrigerate 15 minutes, or until firm.

3 Toss patties in flour, shake off excess. Cook patties on hot, lightly greased barbecue flatplate 2–3 minutes each side until browned and cooked through. Serve with herbed mayonnaise and a green salad, if desired.

4 To make herbed mayonnaise: Combine mayonnaise, herbs and capers in a small bowl; mix well.

Process fish until smooth paste, then add other patty ingredients.

Toss patties in flour and shake off any excess.

Combine mayonnaise, herbs and capers and serve with patties.

Thai Marinated Fish

PREPARATION TIME: 10 minutes
+ 3 hours marinating
TOTAL COOKING TIME: 15 minutes
SERVES 4

1 medium-sized white-fleshed fish, cleaned
  and scaled
25 g (¾ cup) fresh coriander (cilantro) leaves
2 garlic cloves, crushed
1 tablespoon soy sauce
1 tablespoon fish sauce
1 tablespoon sweet chilli sauce
2 teaspoons sesame oil
3 spring onions (scallions), finely chopped
2 teaspoons grated fresh ginger
1 tablespoon lime juice
1 teaspoon soft brown sugar

1 Place fish in large, shallow non-metal dish. Fill fish cavity with coriander leaves.

2 Combine garlic, soy, fish and chilli sauces, oil, spring onions, ginger, juice and sugar in jug; mix well. Pour marinade over fish. Cover and refrigerate several hours or overnight. Prepare and heat the barbecue 1 hour before cooking.

3 Cook fish on hot, lightly greased flatplate for about 15 minutes, taking care not to burn skin of fish. (Move fish away from the flame and dampen the fire if fish begins to stick to plate.) Brush fish frequently with marinade until flesh flakes back easily with a fork, and has turned opaque. Serve with egg noodles and barbecued citrus wedges, if desired.

Fill fish cavity with coriander leaves.

Pour marinade over fish and refrigerate for several hours.

Brush fish frequently with marinade while cooking.

Barbecued Lobster Tails with Avocado Sauce

PREPARATION TIME: 15 minutes
+ 3 hours marinating
TOTAL COOKING TIME: 10 minutes
SERVES 4

60 ml (¼ cup) dry white wine
1 tablespoon honey
1 teaspoon sambal oelek (bottled chopped
  chillies)
1 garlic clove, crushed
1 tablespoon olive oil
4 (400 g/14 oz) fresh raw lobster tails

Avocado sauce
1 medium ripe avocado, mashed
3 teaspoons lemon juice
2 tablespoons sour cream
1 small tomato, chopped finely
salt and pepper, to taste

1 Combine wine, honey, sambal oelek, garlic and oil in jug; mix well.

2 Use a sharp knife or kitchen scissors to cut along the soft shell on the underside of the lobster. Gently pull shell apart and ease raw flesh out with fingers.

3 Place lobster in shallow non-metal dish. Pour over marinade; stir well. Cover, refrigerate several hours or overnight. Prepare and light barbecue 1 hour before cooking. Cook lobster tails on hot lightly greased barbecue grill or flatplate 5–10 minutes, turning frequently. Brush with marinade until cooked through. Slice into medallions and serve with avocado sauce and a green salad, if desired.

4 To make avocado sauce: Combine avocado, juice and sour cream in bowl; mix well. Add tomato and combine with avocado mixture; add salt and pepper, to taste.

Cut along underside of lobster shell and pull raw flesh from shell.

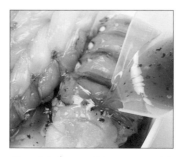
Place lobster meat in a non-metal dish and pour over marinade.

Combine avocado, juice and sour cream; add tomato and season.

Marinated Grilled Vegetables

PREPARATION TIME: 30 minutes
+ 1 hour marinating
TOTAL COOKING TIME: 5 minutes
SERVES 6

3 small slender eggplants (aubergines)
2 small red capsicums (peppers)
3 medium zucchinis (courgettes)
6 medium mushrooms

Marinade
60 ml (¼ cup) olive oil
60 ml (¼ cup) lemon juice
15 g (¼ cup) shredded basil leaves
1 garlic clove, crushed

1 Cut eggplant into diagonal slices. Place on tray in single layer; sprinkle with salt and let stand 15 minutes. Rinse thoroughly and pat dry with paper towels.

2 Trim capsicum, removing seeds and membrane; cut into long, wide pieces. Cut zucchini into diagonal slices. Trim each mushroom stalk so that it is level with the cap. Place all vegetables in a large, shallow non-metal dish.

3 To make marinade: Place oil, juice, basil and garlic in a small screwtop jar. Shake vigorously to combine. Pour over vegetables and combine well. Store, covered with plastic wrap, in refrigerator for 1 hour, stirring occasionally. Prepare and heat barbecue.

4 Place vegetables on hot, lightly greased barbecue grill or flatplate. Cook each vegetable piece over the hottest part of the fire 2 minutes each side. Transfer to a serving dish once browned. Brush vegetables frequently with any remaining marinade while cooking.

Remove seeds and membrane from capsicum and cut into pieces.

Combine marinade ingredients and pour over vegetables.

Cook vegetables over hottest part of grill, brushing with marinade.

Barbecued Mushrooms

PREPARATION TIME: 10 minutes
TOTAL COOKING TIME: 5 minutes
SERVES 6

6 large mushrooms
50 g (1¾ oz) butter, melted
2 garlic cloves, crushed
2 tablespoons finely chopped fresh chives
1 tablespoon fresh thyme leaves
50 g (½ cup) shredded Parmesan cheese

1 Prepare and heat barbecue. Carefully peel skin from mushroom caps. Remove stalks. Combine butter and garlic in a small bowl.

2 Brush tops of mushrooms with garlic butter, place top-side down on hot barbecue flatplate and cook over the hottest part of the fire 2 minutes, or until tops have browned. Turn mushrooms over. Brush upturned bases with garlic butter; cook 2 minutes.

3 Sprinkle bases with combined chives and thyme, then cheese, and cook a further 3 minutes, until cheese begins to melt. Serve immediately.

Peel skin from mushroom caps and remove stalks.

Brush tops of mushrooms with garlic butter.

Sprinkle base of mushrooms with cheese, chives and thyme.

Chickpea Salad

PREPARATION TIME: 20 minutes
TOTAL COOKING TIME: Nil or 2 hours
30 minutes (if using dried peas)
SERVES 6 8

370 g (1¾ cups) dried chickpeas or 2 large
  cans chickpeas
3½ litres (14 cups) water
60 ml (¼ cup) olive oil
1 medium red onion
3 medium tomatoes
1 small red capsicum (pepper)
4 spring onions (scallions)
60 g (1 cup) chopped fresh parsley
2–3 tablespoons chopped fresh mint leaves

Dressing
2 tablespoons tahini (sesame paste)
2 tablespoons fresh lemon juice
2 tablespoons water
60 ml (¼ cup) olive oil
2 garlic cloves, crushed
½ teaspoon ground cumin
salt and pepper, to taste

1 If using dried chickpeas, place in medium pan. Cover with water and oil. Bring to the boil, partially cover and cook on medium heat 2½ hours or until tender. (Chickpeas will cook in about 30 minutes in a pressure cooker.)

2 Pour chickpeas into colander. Rinse thoroughly with cold water and set aside to drain. If using canned chickpeas, drain well, rinse and drain again.

3 Peel the onion; slice thinly. Cut tomatoes in half; remove seeds with a spoon. Cut tomato flesh into small pieces. Slice capsicum and spring onions into long thin strips. Combine onion, tomatoes, capsicum and spring onion in a bowl. Add the cooled chickpeas, parsley and mint.

4 To make dressing: Combine tahini, juice, water, oil, garlic, cumin, salt and pepper in a screwtop jar and shake vigorously to make a creamy liquid. Pour over the salad; mix through.

Drain chickpeas and rinse thoroughly with cold water.

Cut tomatoes in half and remove seeds; cut flesh into small pieces.

Place dressing ingredients in a screwtop jar and shake vigorously.

Barbecued Corn on the Cob with Tomato Relish

PREPARATION TIME: 15 minutes
TOTAL COOKING TIME: 1 hour
SERVES 6

Tomato relish
400 g (14 oz) can peeled tomatoes
170 ml (⅔ cup) white vinegar
125 ml (½ cup) white sugar
1 garlic clove, finely chopped
2 spring onions (scallions), finely chopped
4 sun-dried tomatoes, finely chopped
1 small fresh red chilli, finely chopped
½ teaspoon salt
½ teaspoon cracked black pepper

6 large cobs fresh corn
1–2 tablespoons olive or vegetable oil
60 g (2¼ oz) butter
salt to taste

1 Prepare and heat barbecue. To make tomato relish: Roughly chop tomatoes or process briefly in a food processor bowl. Combine vinegar and sugar in medium pan. Stir over medium heat until sugar dissolves. Bring to boil. Reduce heat and simmer 2 minutes; add tomatoes, garlic, spring onions, sun-dried tomatoes and chilli. Bring to the boil, reduce heat and simmer 35 minutes, stirring frequently.

2 Add salt and pepper and continue to cook until relish has thickened. Remove from the heat and allow to cool.

3 Brush the corn with oil and cook on the hot, lightly greased barbecue grill 5 minutes, each side, until corn is soft and cobs are flecked with brown in places. Using tongs, lift the corn onto the flatplate and moisten each with a square of butter. Sprinkle with salt. Serve at once with tomato relish.

Add chilli to tomato relish and simmer for 35 minutes.

Add salt and pepper and continue to cook until sauce thickens.

Brush corn with oil and barbecue until kernels are soft.

75

Red Potato Salad

PREPARATION TIME: 20 minutes
TOTAL COOKING TIME: 10 minutes
SERVES 8

1.25 kg (2 lb 12 oz) red potatoes
1 medium red onion
2 teaspoons oil
3 rashers bacon, finely chopped
185 ml (¾ cup) whole egg mayonnaise
185 ml (¾ cup) plain yoghurt
3 spring onions (scallions), finely chopped

1 Scrub potatoes thoroughly and cut into 3 cm (1¼ inch) pieces. Cook potatoes in large pan of boiling water 5 minutes, or until just tender. Drain and cool completely. Cut onion in half and slice finely. Heat oil in frying pan. Cook bacon 5 minutes or until well browned and crisp. Drain on paper towel.

2 Place potatoes, bacon and onion in a large mixing bowl. Combine mayonnaise, yoghurt and spring onions in a small mixing bowl, pour over potato mixture.

3 Fold through gently, taking care not to break up potatoes. Transfer to a large serving bowl and serve at room temperature.

Cut onion in half and slice finely.

Combine dressing ingredients and pour over potato and onion mix.

Fold through gently taking care not to break up the potatoes.

Snowpea Salad

PREPARATION TIME: 10 minutes
TOTAL COOKING TIME: Nil
SERVES 6–8

150 g (5½ oz) snowpeas (mangetout)
1 bunch fresh asparagus
2 medium carrots, peeled
425 g (15 oz) can baby corn, drained
230 g (8 oz) can bamboo shoots, drained

Dressing
60 ml (¼ cup) vegetable oil
3 teaspoons sesame oil
1 tablespoon soy sauce

1 To make dressing: Place oils and sauce in a small screwtop jar; shake well to combine.

2 Trim snowpeas; cut in half. Remove woody ends from asparagus and cut asparagus into 5 cm (2 inch) lengths. Cut carrots into matchsticks.

3 Place snowpeas and asparagus in a heatproof bowl and cover with boiling water. Stand 1 minute, drain and plunge into iced water. Drain and dry thoroughly on paper towels.

4 Combine snowpeas, asparagus, carrots, corn and bamboo shoots in serving bowl. Pour on dressing. Serve with garlic bread, if desired.

Trim snowpeas and cut in half. Cut carrot into matchsticks.

Place snowpeas and asparagus in bowl and cover with boiling water.

Combine vegetables in a bowl and pour dressing over.

All our recipes are thoroughly tested in a specially developed test kitchen. Standard metric measuring cups and spoons are used in the development of our recipes. All cup and spoon measurements are level. We have used 60 g (2¼ oz/Grade 3) eggs in all recipes. Sizes of cans vary from manufacturer to manufacturer and between countries – use the can size closest to the one suggested in the recipe.

CONVERSION GUIDE

1 cup = 250 ml (9 fl oz)

1 teaspoon = 5 ml

1 Australian tablespoon = 20 ml (4 teaspoons)

1 UK/US tablespoon = 15 ml (3 teaspoons)

Where temperature ranges are indicated, the lower figure applies to gas ovens, the higher to electric ovens. This allows for the fact that the flame in gas ovens generates a drier heat, which effectively cooks food faster than the moister heat of an electric oven, even if the temperature setting is the same.

DRY MEASURES	LIQUID MEASURES	LINEAR MEASURES
30 g = 1 oz	30 ml = 1 fl oz	6 mm = ¼ inch
250 g = 9 oz	125 ml = 4 fl oz	1 cm = ½ inch
500 g = 1 lb 2 oz	250 ml = 9 fl oz	2.5 cm = 1 inch

CUP CONVERSIONS – DRY INGREDIENTS

1 cup almonds, slivered whole = 125 g (4½ oz)

1 cup cheese, lightly packed processed cheddar = 155 g (5½oz)

1 cup wheat flour = 125 g (4½ oz)

1 cup wholemeal flour = 140 g (5 oz)

1 cup minced (ground) meat = 250 g (9 oz)

1 cup pasta shapes = 125 g (4½ oz)

1 cup raisins = 170 g (6 oz)

1 cup rice, short grain, raw = 200 g (7 oz)

1 cup sesame seeds = 160 g (6 oz)

1 cup split peas = 250 g (9 oz)

	°C	°F	GAS MARK
Very slow	120	250	½
Slow	150	300	2
Mod slow	160	325	3
Moderate	180	350	4
Mod hot	190(g)–210(e)	375–425	5
Hot	200(g)–240(e)	400–475	6
Very hot	230(g)–260(e)	450–525	8

(g) = gas (e) = electric

Note: For fan-forced ovens, check your appliance manual, but as a general rule, set the oven temperature to 20°C lower than the temperature indicated in the recipe.

INTERNATIONAL GLOSSARY

capsicum	sweet bell pepper	cornflour	cornstarch
chick pea	garbanzo bean	eggplant	aubergine
chilli	chile, chili pepper	spring onion	scallion
		zucchini	courgette

First published in 2008 by Murdoch Books Pty Limited,
Erico House, 6th Floor North, 93-99 Upper Richmond Road, Putney, London SW15 2TG.

This edition published 2008 for Index Books Ltd

ISBN 978 1 74196 1799

Printed by Sing Cheong Printing Co. Ltd. Printed in China.